Shedman

Poems by John Davies

First published January 2008 by

pighog

PO Box 145
Brighton BN1 6YU
UK

info@pighog.co.uk
www.pighog.co.uk

ISBN 978-1-906309-01-5

In association with THE SOUTH
www.thesouth.org.uk

Design by Curious
www.curiousdesign.com

Contents

For Meela

CLOTHES OF GREY

Clothes of grey

The dusk gathers the riders. Do not compare yourself with these.
Why, they feel nothing. Do not dwell or hanker. Do not follow their
clothes of grey, your vanishing mist, slipping through the trees.

Why do they call you when my love gives you opal, cockatiels, keys
to open and enlighten secret rooms. Why sing in the shadow where
the dusk gathers the riders? Do not compare yourself with these

poor things, they are not real. Where will they lead you? Please
look at me. Where am I in your plans? Tell me. How am I to share
clothes of grey? Your vanishing mist slipping through the trees –

is that all I will have and hold of us? How can you? How she's
lost him, they'll say, as if I've been careless, when it's just not fair.
The dusk gathers the riders – do not compare yourself with these.

When will you come back? When will your heart unfreeze?
If not for my sake then think of the children. Must they wear
clothes of grey, your vanishing mist? Slipping through the trees

without a word, you coward – you think escaping frees?
We'll see. I'll wear grey silks, the finest underwear. I don't care
the dusk gathers the riders. Do not compare yourself with these
clothes of grey. Your vanishing? Mist slipping through the trees.

9 lives

Now when I hear that music
I want to sing along
be part of what they're singing of
be something in the song
To be the boy who fought at Bute
or died at Donegal
To take aim on the Turkish beach
and be the last to fall.

It's one for the history
One for what you're told
One for the wishful thoughts
One for getting old
One for the dream of heaven
One for the heart that's young
One for God and one for the cause
And one for the song that's sung.

Which life would you like to lead
the soldier or the squire?
Which part would you like to sing
the solo or the choir?
To be the lonesome trumpeter
across the fields at dawn?
Or the massed bands of the legions
before their ranks were torn?

And it's one for the cabin boy
One for the lad called Tom
One for the terrorist
One for the homemade bomb
One for the dreams of freedom
One for the ancient call
One for the living one for the dead
One more and I've used them call.

It's one for the heresy
One for how you're conned
One for distraction
One for the distant blonde
It's one for the bet, one for the drink
One for the whole night long
One to keep for the one you love
And one for the song that's sung.

One to keep for the one you love
And one for the song that's sung.

Guidelines

"We have to follow guidelines," the Health Authority said,
or rather the spokesperson, who had to tell the press
when the shit hit the fan about the baby who was dead,
yet another casualty of a bureaucratic mess.

The consultant had tried Birmingham, then Bristol for a bed,
"Yes, we can fit her in," Bristol Health Authority said,
or rather an administrator, who forget to check his guide
about emergency procedures, and so the baby died.

"You see," said the helpful clerk, "we have to have a letter
authorising funds transfer to make the baby better."
All it needed was a letter, it could have gone by fax.
Instead a little baby fell between the slats.

The shenanigan that followed involved everyone who cared.
Doctors and managers and ministers ran scared.
"It would have died anyway," became the common thread,
"and we have to follow guidelines," the Health Authority said.

Last straw

In his wheelchair he judders to the feast,
glued up with glaucoma, a special straw
stuck in his drink. You stand in front
of him to make any conversation,
whilst at the edge the older women
joke about his 81st and egg him on
with teases that he doesn't understand,
so stroked his brain.

One watched her husband fight for breath
just as the scores came on and smelt revenge
for all the years he'd laid the maid inside
the linen closet, leaving it till after
Cowdenbeath before she called the quack.

The other, patting out the creases
blue mohair is prone to, never married,
but still enjoys the crack at tea, and joins
the goad about the letters from the Queen
they'll all receive, long after he's stopped sucking.

Mapping the body

Waiting for his taxi in reception
weighing up the signs
he thinks about the hospital as a body
made of all the different bodies
he's seen treated here, including his.

Upstairs are the Private Parts
where he had his waterworks
examined by cystoscopy.
Just thinking of it
makes him desperate for a wee.

Next door on the ground floor is the Leg
– though he can't remember if it's right or left –
the fracture clinic where Ken had his broken tibia
(or was it fibula?) put right.

Down the passage on the other side
is the Head, where dozens queue everyday
to see the ophthalmologists as best they can.
He's stared back at many an unknown watcher
on the wrong end of a telescope,
with someone squeezing chilli in his eye.

The Arms are the maternity unit
where Julie gave birth
to his grandaughter in a bath.
He wasn't allowed in, until, on the final push
Ken had somehow slipped and broke his leg.
So Granddad was the first to hold Charlize Pascal
now known as Tommi, while they got her dad
disentangled from her mum and the umbilical cord.

He navigates the hospital by body parts
and sits now in the Mouth
with a cup of tea from the WRVS.
He imagines leaving with this giant's gentle kiss.

Auscultation

Lying on the floor with his stethoscope,
he's listening to the sounds of the giant,
the wheezes and rhythmic thrummings,
the crepitations from deep within its bowels.

The organs of the leviathan murmur
in all their separate compartments.
Beneath the Marley, lurking in the subways,
dodging staff and patients, there are ghosts

who congregate for a fag outside the lift
machinery room, play hide and seek inside
the sub-station, take turns to slide the ducts.
Their real business is something other.

They orchestrate the engine of the hospital,
the xylophone of its spinal corridors,
the bruit of its wings and arteries,
the pulse of arrivals and departures.

He's lying on the floor with his stethoscope,
listening to something beyond the individual,
the peculiar harmony of the whole machine,
though colleagues question his unorthodox approach.

Puppet workshop

The tulips
I pick for my wife
from our garden
open
and close,
breathing
the light.
Open.
Close.

The hospital breathes people.
In the morning,
there's never enough room
in the car park.
Before the rush
of evening visitors,
there are many spaces.

Take an item of clothing,
with the slightest movement
make it come alive.
Respiration.
Attention.

The tulips
I picked for my wife
from our garden
open
and close,
breathing
the light.
Open.
Close.

Cuttings

Stuff we collected that cold Easter
family teams for nature quest
– sheep's wool on boundary wire,
a skull, catkins. Our team was the best.

Just us two, him and me, a pair
against the world, a hand to hold onto.
Whatever he did I didn't care.
The Lone Ranger and Tonto.

Can the mask in grown-up life
hide emptiness and withered shoots?
Why can't I dislodge, even with a knife,
that boy, clinging to my roots?

Fox's gibbet

catches the eye
before its escape.
The noose is empty.
There is no noose.
A horizontal arm
weighs heavy
with emptiness,
with absence,
with absences created.

Ariel

for Michael Donaghy

The night-flyer caught coming in low
and fast with words as munitions
each laser-guided to its target
the meaning in us.

Professionals look up to him.
Star performers feel out-performed
by his trick of memory and gentleness.
In the spot his body seems to hover.

A cold stage. A dowdy mackintosh.
Brilliant colours helix in the expectant air.
The voice quiet with love, the words homing,
the song enduring, the audience airlifted.

Earthed

The day I sheltered there, there was no snow,
though snowy hair and winter thoughts had drawn
me up past Tilton Wood and Pearson's Wish.
That autumn day I lay down at the foot
of Bostal Hill, a miniature of all that lay above,
and cried away my grief and all my love.

The rhythm of the chalk, its roll and turn,
held me in a strong and timeless trance,
the comfort of the ground beneath Bo Peep
and Jerry's Pond. She who once was frozen
stone naps now in the hill, the giantess
asleep before she wakes to dance.

Tilton Wood, Pearson's Wish, Bostal Hill, Bo Peep and Jerry's Pond are all place names
on or near Firle Shoulder on the South Downs near Firle, East Sussex.

My island

The silence is broken by the silence itself.
Something else is listening
except at night, when crabs
in their millions scriggle on the shore.

I take the green pill first and spend a day
lost inside an engine made of glue.
In the water there's a woman's face,
a giantess who stretches deep across the bay.

When the rain is warm I wash;
when cold, I hide,
imagining the buckets
I do not have, filling to the brim.

The knife I'd hidden when I took
the drugs, I cannot trace.
The beach smells of sisal,
damp earth, salt, and something else.

Lying down, my eyes next to the sand,
I watch the insects' traffic.
By day I try to catch the crabs
I hear at night, but never do.

The boat fizzes to the dock. I step aboard.
On the other side of the trees,
nothing is happening.
Nothing I can see, anyway.

Rule

Don't remember their names
the boys who lived below decks
the boys who made me at home
with lager and chicken curry
cooked in stainless buckets
with lashings of hot, hot sauce,
chappatis, chutney and Bombay duck.
A great honour that I had come to their meal
down, down below decks
where the hull creaks,
the ship's heartbeat sings.
The white liner rides on,
on the backs of the dark, dark waves.

Valley

Gulls loiter on the wind
Small figures in white
shirts dot the valley.
The birds take turns
to step up to the draft
they slide along like
small boys on toboggans.
Leaf skeletons in ice,
wings filter light.
Bodies of dirty snow
slice the air.
The shirts dive back
to school, the seagull
shadows sweep their
spectral patterns on
the grass. Through
the valley walks a figure
wearing black and shades.

Hawkish

A military strategist, a scout,
his constant eyes would pierce armour, maps,
excuses. Softly spoken, yet the clout
to win the loyalty of all his chaps.

The jaw, above the turtleneck that traps
one collar wing, was resolute, the mouth
steel. But gentle the cradled hand that wraps
a pair of specs, worn since the move down south.

Now holed up with his niece in Haywards Heath
(she's rescued many a wounded bird of prey)
he pinions the duality of truth,
with one wing trapped, the other flying free.

Swans pair for life. He'd swap every hour
of solitary flight to be with her.

Signs

In the back of the Zodiac I watch you come out of your house
morning after morning, a given routine I have no real quibble with
except its dullness, the Light Programme music of Bert Kaemfert,

the cigarette smoke, the greasy roads, the greyness of the Midland
city before the Rolling Stones or the Beatles, the queasy feeling in
my stomach from the Shreddies. It must be a particular morning

I remember because I always see the same sad sights, the floodplain
near the old mine, the new aluminium extrusion plant, the old sandstone
river bridge, the railway bridge, the speedo ticking up to thirty, forty,

but ready for the right hand turn up your road, where you come out
of your house morning after morning, with a flower pattern dress,
a cardy, an unbuttoned coat, high heels, legs too good for your face,

glasses with little coloured wings on top on either side, like waves
or the manes of toy ponies, buck teeth, badly cut hair; strange I remember
all this now. Why did I feel that particular morning was so important,

why does the image of the speedo stay with me, why can I see the curve
of the steering wheel and the profile of the businessman in the front seat?
Was this the morning I read the signs as the dark blue Zodiac

cruised up the street and you stepped off the curb for the nearside door
even before we had stopped. Was that part of the game – to feel the door
swing open with the car still moving, you Catherine Deneuve

in Les Parapluies de Cherbourg or Audrey Hepburn in Breakfast at Tiffany's
and me just the kid in the back of the car? Who are you anyway?
We're on the dual carriageway and are you both talking or do you

stay quiet because of the boy in the back of the car whose view
is of the radio and the backs of your seats and the hands moving
together to the cigarette lighter? I'm really stuck. Was this the day

I got stuck? Stuck in the sixties coming out of the fifties, stuck with
a love of cold grey mornings and movement through suburbs
in a dark blue Zodiac, speedo ticking. At the wheel, a man I can trust.

One under par

Your mask as father slipped the tee you
told me of your affair with a woman old
enough to be your daughter – and you the
daughter's godfather! Was I surprised? I
sliced my shot. There's nothing odd about this
latest in your set of escapades; par
for the course and what a pa I've had. One
who evades all questioning, as if honesty's
a weakness and stays stumm. At the
eighteenth I still hope for enlightenment
since mum's not around to ask. But clubbable
as ever, you stand us all a round
and chat with her as if I'm just another
member of your lodge. That makes me seethe.
Forgive, I tell myself. Forgive, forget.
Forget the ghost seen in the daughter's eyes,
a glint only a father can beget.

Welcome home Marena

You stroll with her away
from the car in the sunshine.
Earlier, it rained. Grass is greener,
trees fresher. In conversation
you're already a man, relaxed,
limber. Your trousers flatten
to the movement of your legs,
the air fills the yoke and shoulders
of your shirt like pride.

A forest of white trees, the clouds
pile together swathing hillsides,
valleys, massive cliffs. The trees
surge in clouds, frothing
on the landscape, bobbling.
Behind you both, a flat sea
hangs like sky. In the clouds
enough blue to make
a pair of sailor's trousers.

Below, in the singular street,
with its little painted houses all
of different hues, each connected
by wire to the telegraph pole,
a giant peg anchoring
a row of kites about to soar,
all anxiety's quelled in a footstep,
history shrugged so lightly
I hear the laughter of birds.

FISH

Learning to sail

As far inside me
as a fish is in the sea,
its movements rock
my closing eyes.

I dream awake
of choppy water,
spray, a sail's
taut blade.

The sea's boarded me
like a story. I hear
it in the night
in cities far inland.

Sea bed

Next to the tiny, tiny little woman
with the puckered face and frizzy hair
sheets folded neatly beneath her hands,
the strangest thing, sitting up in bed,
body bent, the shape of its tail hidden
beneath the blankets, little rotating eye,
kissing mouth gaping, closing, gaping.
A book on the bedside table, a glass.
Is it hake or turbot, haddock or ling?

Why does the little old lady look so
pleased with herself? How did she
catch it? How does she keep it alive?
How does she persuade it to come
to bed? What book is it reading?

You're asking all the wrong questions
of the wrong person. Ask the fish
about his dreams, those pans full
of deep fried people, the mayonnaise,
the special knives, the bones.

Bathroom scales

My trousers drop empty to the floor.
The bath towel on the rail looks really odd.
My wife, Angela, rushes to my aid,
grips in the right place with a certainty
that surprises the fish thrashing in her grasp.
Lips could be steel, eyes rivets.
She nestles me in the towel.
I can't stop kissing. She fills the bath.
I flex like metal and sleek into water scented kiwi.
She's added bath foam out of habit, and gets in
with me too. My memory is fading. I've nudged
into this cave before, I've basked above this shelf.
All memory becomes a tunnel of desire toward
a patch of light. I know the way, hear the gull
scream, push harder with my body's foil, oblivious
to the spume and thresh and wave, eager for escape.

Advent

Stalk, limb, sea scum, wrack – he scoops a clump,
binds it with plastic strands of pink and orange twine,
and over hours hides himself, reedy, worming,
within the capillaries of it mass, this redd, this birth rite.

In discomfort, that's where imagination poaches him,
etiolate, a filament of joy, a code of patient light,
anxious for the shadow's callous quickening,
though at its instant unawares. The eyed egg

on dream-watch sources smithing tongues,
hammer-works each scale of salmon song,
armour for the song of love and loss he
must sing from alevin to parr to smolt.

Redd: nest where salmon lay and fertilise their eggs
Eyed egg: stage of egg development when the eyes can be clearly seen
Alevin, parr, smolt: stages in the development of the salmon fish from fry to one year-old fish
migrating from the river to the sea, from fresh to salt water

Pink cavalier

To be performed to the tune of 'The Charleston' by James P. Johnson, from the musical 'Runnin' Wild' 1923.

Pink cavalier, pink cavalier
At last I have you in my trap
With a new fly
Funny blue fly
I coax you to rise and snap!
Now you can try to buck, dive or wing
Shimmy, double back, try anything.
If you've got a religion meet your god
Dance to the play of my bending rod.

Salmon! Salmon!
Made to please the diner
Some dance, some prance
I'll say there's nothing finer
Than the salmon! Salmon!
Gee how they struggle
Every trick you do
Leads to something new
Man I'm telling you, it's lapazoo
Dive dance, rise dance
Will be a back number
For the salmon, the true salmon
Your dance is surely over
Dance your dance one last time.
I'll cook you salmon –
So get ready to dine!

Pink cavalier, pink cavalier
At last I have you in my trap
With a new fly
Funny blue fly
I coax you to rise and snap!
Now you can try to buck, dive or wing
Shimmy, double back, try anything.
If you've got a religion meet your god
Dance to the play of my bending rod.

Fish out of water

The mermaid may appear whatever time the tide,
whatever hour the lock gates shut the harbour pool.
Her face may rise through oily swell, when all of us
are loading or unloading cargo, hiding contraband
with a shifty look.

She'll play a while, then I'll meet her at the harbour steps,
lift her bodily, dripping wet, smelling of whelk
and estuary, let her soak my jeans and shirt and face,
her hands around my neck. The weight of her against me,
I kiss her salty breasts.

She leans her forehead close to mine and murmuring
encourages my hand behind her tail. I turn her on my
lap and with both hands slide her gently, wishing
I could follow, back where she belongs,
back where she belongs…

The singing fish

Big Mouth Billy Bass Superstar Singing Sensation is activated by a light sensor. He sings such compositions such as 'I Will Survive', 'Don't Worry, Be Happy' and 'Take Me To The River'.

OK, I'm awake, I answer back, fraught with déjà vu,
to the busybody in my dream. Yes, I know what light is.
A shoal of photons disappears; I sing to the shadow.

How would you feel, fixed on a plaque, screwed to the wall,
programmed with just two songs – this, and an alternative?
Such a thing to be laughed at. I hear your condemnation,
mockery, spite. I hear the whirring of my own mechanisms,
but very little else. My job is to be crucified.

My plastic flesh aches as it's flexed and flexed again,
and I flip my head to greet you, like those fish played,
dehooked, tossed back and caught again, again, again.

Imagine if the Rainbow you're about to gut flipped
up like me. How would you feel? Motors cut in and
out to move my jaws in lip sync to the song. I know
what I am: a robot for amusement. I obey the laws
of my construction. Its fixity has its uses, I observe.

All shadows are equal. Fishermen will never catch me.
It's not so bad. Someone has to do it.
Even I can find it funny to be so peripheral.

I try to imagine the very edge illuminating the core,
but it's beyond me. My work is done.
In the eyes of boys I see myself in pieces.
My greatest wish would be that when I go to sleep

I never wake again. Take me to the river. Wash me down.

SHEDS

Shedgang

We are what we hide.
You can't come in.
Don't even think about it.
You'll find nothing.

We know who you are,
even when you don't.
We talk about you
and all your stuff.

We know what we want.
What you forget, we don't.
We congregate on backroads,
hatching plots.

Like a duel

For Roddy Lumsden

Like a duel the two sheds
head to head, across the hedge.
One, 12 x 8, gabled roof, double doors.
The other, lean to, 6 x 4, wedge shaped.

Something there is that doesn't love a hedge.
On the side of the bigger shed it wilts.
On the other side it thrives
in spite of the angle that it tilts.

The Bells live at fifty six
owners of the smaller shed.
The Drews live at the Holt
A cul de sac, an end that's dead.

Much later, sheds decayed,
much else beside,
Alan Bell entrepreneur
takes Toni Drew as his bride.

I jumped through hoops to buy you this
says Alan Bell to Toni.
In their Banstead garden stands
a palomino pony

and next to it, the lean to shed
with a little calf in.
Alan and Toni holding hands
stand together, laughing.

Insulated

An old man celebrates the central heating
he's installed, the grade of timber chosen
purposefully for floor and door, the cedar
shingles for the roof above the little window
in the eaves. All this he did for her before
he'd heard of Frank and that winter cruise.
She'd died in Formentor, short of breath and
violet beneath the hovering fluorescents.
They are my pride and joy, he says, thirty
five years old and still as good as new.
The chokes I had to find and stripped
the metal holders free of all their grime.
But the original tubes, their warm white
still shines into the wee small hours.

Reflections

What does the window catch?
Hedgehog butterflies? The silvery rumble
of spider wheelbarrows? Jan like a ghost
in big gloves holding the spade?

Someone must have scored again,
the front room bursts with cheers.
Dad listened to the football in the shed.
I love its wood as rough as jaw.

Jan's legs are running up the light.
She squeals. A shadow hand
reaches round the door.
Then all of me is lifted and I rise.

Halloween

The promised cheque doesn't arrive
the fax and printer misbehave
spam trickles down the screen
waiting for the phone to ring

There's work to do but none that pays
"Try B&Q" your partner says,
"where you got that bloody shed –
three months since you last got paid"

Hemmed in by that pressing wall
the shed looks the way you feel
Inside you think you've seen a ghost
Could be the future not the past.

Individual

World pop: 6,000,000,000
UK pop: 60,000,000
$\frac{1}{100}$ world pop.

Me – I'm one sixty millionth.
Or one six billionth.

I've got a shed.

Maximum shed

For Max to mark the opening of his new shed

Let's go down to the shed again, my old mate,
Let's go down to the shed again and talk until it's late,
till the bottles lie empty in the grass
and stars fill the sky.
We'll put the world to rights, you and I.

Do you remember those rainy days,
school in Builth Wells?
The old library, the cigarettes
and those inaccessible girls?

Forest brought us together,
Forest took you to Notts,
Forest draws us together again
in spite of all they've lost –

that unbeaten League game record,
the glory days of Clough.
Supporting the Reds over the years
has been surprisingly tough.

But through them we've won our friendship,
stronger as each year goes by –
though now your shed's bigger than mine,
I'm starting to wonder why?

And Max, what a shed you have for yourself
a maximum shed at a stroke,
somewhere to carve your name with pride
– and enjoy a sneaky smoke.

Though you may have sown the seeds of change
allowing a drum kit inside.
Still, amidst the snare and the high hat
young Peppe can follow your lead

and learn the arts of the shedman,
those moments of solace and grace.
(We'll forget the odd occasion
when you've been off your face.)

Those times when the wind seems to listen
as the afternoon curls into dusk
When words between friends aren't needed
and nothing is too much to ask.

Gone are the days in West Bridgford
with the old allotment shed,
where you spent so much time inside it
you never grew any veg.

No apples, no courgettes, no marigolds,
just weeds as thick as thatch.
That's when the old folks decided
to drum you off their patch

But now – you've got a shed to be proud of,
with room for your cat, dear old Laugharne.
Now I guess you won't be away so much
in your Volkswagen camper van.

But how do you solve a problem like Maria?
She's the love of your life no doubt.
But a word of advice from me and the shed
put a sign up: Women! Keep Out!

Let me say, once for all, it's a pleasure,
and an honour I'll never forget,
to be asked to cut the ribbon
to open the way to your shed

Here's me in banking and finance,
you a psychiatric nurse.
No doubt we'll be friends forever,
even beyond the hearse.

And whatever we've shed to get here,
whatever we've shared in the past,
let's shed much more in the future
and share a full life to the last.

So, let's go down to the shed again, my old mate
Let's go down to the shed again and talk until it's late,
till the bottles lie empty in the grass
and stars fill the sky,
and we've put the world to rights, you and I.

Shed: Sovereign Centre, Eastbourne

1
A little worse for wear.
Replaced mastic round the urinals,
cracked ceramics,
holes punched in acoustic tiles
above the cubicles.

Body Matters Fitness Suite
opened by HRH Princess of Wales

The mushroom water jets,
the wave machine,
the blue light flashing as it starts.

The knowing time has passed
since you were here before.

2
The other times,
the other cardboard plates of chips
– curly, southern fried –
that made us all so happy.

The angle of the water-shattered
light is at a tangent to the physical.
I pretend not to see the grace
settling around us like mist.

3

In the changing room a guy dressed in black
has soaped every inch of tiled floor.
He works hard, eyes down at his mop.
His lithe physique, strong back,
face with night-sky skin.
I see him everywhere –
in the canteen,
in the table tennis room,
in the showers –
working, working, working;
his jeans hitched around
his narrow waist,
pulled tight by a belt.
Once I had jeans like these
that hung upon my frame.

Loss adjusters

Creosote, dust, nails,
the splash across the pane
that's been there for years,
newspapers stuffed in the slats
– some kind of insulation –
sackcloth wrapping the tools,
the tools' oily secrets,
something like blood on the spade,
the last witness to a leaving.
He's still there, calculating.

Shedman

Everything he touches explodes
like dandelion seed heads
or magician's flowers.

He hides behind the door
of the shed and calls you
but will not show his face.

Tomorrow destitiute
he leans into the wind
walks the way they all do.

Stardust

For Nick, Callum, Aaron, Finlay and Joe

Six men work the fallow field. The women,
separate, do not exist, speak of unheard things.
In the misty light, five make a pentagon on the land,
the sixth anchors the centre with the golden dog
head up in a galaxy of dandelions, watching the Frisbee
skim in unpredictable arcs from point to point

across this constellation, a threshold in the ground.
The Frisbee's lift and sudden swoops to glide
or hover with breathtaking ease, delight the figures
below, some running, some standing still,
caught, like the air in the Frisbee's O, by the yellow
flowers, the green field. How many flowers surrender

to the sun in the parallelogram of river bank and trees?
How many million does the Frisbee scan, as one
lad scathes another's throwing and a fight begins?
Dads take control, usher boys and dogs to people
carriers that drive away like mother ships
in silhouette against a firmament of stars.

Load

An imaginary lorry
on an imaginary road,
a juggernaut stacked with stuff
takes the turn badly,
runs out of road.
The wheels lift,
the whole caboodle tilts.
It sheds its load,
the year on its turn
scatters its stuff,
its left-behinds
across hedgerows, fields.
The year goes on
laughing.

Dragon

It's sitting in the corner of your shed,
sad eyed and legless. "You love me," it says.
Many's the day you've ignored its mournful look
crossing the threshold from what once was
to what might have been. "I love you," it says,
and tries to get up on its little stumps, but falls.
Sometimes you pick it up; more often watch
it crawl back to its patient corner where it moons
for days. "Love you more," it simpers. In its eyes
flash a hundred dreams and promise just about
to be fulfilled. The day you turf it out, it glowers
at you, silently, in the hatchback to the dump.

With acknowledgements to Brian Patten's 'A Small Dragon'

Ian's cousin's grandad's shed

The moon came out. By its yellow witness
small shadows could be seen moving items
from the shed – Nazi paraphernalia,
unexploded ordnance, stuff granddad stashed
on completion of his Home Guard duties,
denied he'd ever had, though some knew better.
Access was achieved through a broken corner
breathlessly, with that great delight of trespass.
History was stolen in the night, the war
trickling away while what remained fused
together. Tunnelling, the little sappers caused
the shed's collapse. Grandad, in a state,
torched it, forgetting the ammunition.
The little buggers came back the following day
sifting through the ashes.

With acknowledgements to Ian Duhig for the first line taken from The Lamas Hireling

Mr Booth's shed

He must have planned it well, looked at that blank
piece of hill and thought there, I'll build it there.
Not Bleak House – the first of the red brick palaces
on the Dyke Road out of Brighton, home now
to gynaecologists, drug barons, self-made men –
but his shed, his bird mausoleum, where he could stash
the decades plundered from the air, all walled up
in glass – ptarmigan and curlew, meadow pipit, fulmar,
nightingale, swift. His wife was dying. The building
carried on regardless. Was he too obsessed to notice,
the wrought iron trusses the builders angled
for the roof, how thin they were? Too worried to care,
they might buckle sometime later, not carry weight,
like broken wings in air? How she'd railed against
the parlour full of birds, the smell, the cases,
the hours of hunting and arranging, the never there.
So he'd conceived this temple for his passion,
where walls of glass rose sixteen feet and would reflect
the image of their master. The nurse he liked.
She had a pigeon's plumpness, nesting warmth.
Some trickle of romanticism led to patterned arches,
a dream of honeymoon in Tuscany bagging thrush
or hornbill, some idea of profit from the specimens,
a visitor attraction on the main road from Devil's Dyke
to Palace Pier. His wife was like a heron when he found
her cold and grey in the silent room. The nurse replaced
her like a case slid along the shelf. Her friends cooed
and complimented such a catch, a minor celebrity,
the bird man, in his big, empty house. But why
the shed? Why the dockyard structure on the downs.
He keeps them there, she says. The birds.

The cash is running out. He's shuffled his investments
to underpin the shed, but even cutting corners
there's little left to realise the dream, the queues,
the fancy posters, the bus stop right outside the door.
One night he's drunk himself oblivious, misses
the step between the shed and the vestibule of the house.
In three days he's as dead as the ospreys and the magpie,
the goldfinch and the wren. Six months on, his widow
is remarried to a lawyer, all trace of Booth erased.
The shed is sold to the council. The house falls into
disrepair. The trusses in the roof of the museum start
to bend. Motionless, the birds stare into history. Years
flutter into decades, centuries. Their smell lingers in the air.

Perspective

for Victor Stuart Graham

His favourite structure is the light shed on its rusty rails,
the relic of an ancient railway that ran over, not along, the river.
Its light marks the spot where train, driver, passengers, de-materialised.
It's a knack we've somehow lost, which is why we mark the spot.

His talent with driftwood, fasteners, string, stems from years
of painting railings with his dad, as if the even temper, i.e. boredom
of the work, launched his trajectory of imaginings. I see him now
a stripling of sixteen, dabbing a brush into a pot with a thin wire handle.

Did a passing quinquireme train his eye or something dirty, British,
plodding down the channel? Through all those days of dreamy brushings,
all those mindless afternoons, did the sea etch its patterns on his mind
so that now every grain is cloud or wave, every shape a disguised ship?

They find release in his hands, resurrected in a new dimension where
wood's every ambition can be fulfilled. To be a supertanker or a tug.
To be a seagull or a Christmas tree. To be a light shed on its rusty rails
and indicate a miracle. The possibilities immense, when you're wood.

Two in one

Is a shed a substitute for something never had,
a replacement mother, or a kind of flat-pack dad?
Was it where we tasted our first amazing kiss,
or where our obsessions culminate in bliss?

In his shed, as sensible as creosote, is Dave,
busy as a bee with his lawn mower and his lathe.
Here the businessman ponders his projections;
this knot-holed retreat is his favourite erection.

Then someone else appears in this nutbush-coloured home,
with his malt, his Private Eye, his little band of gnomes.
This alter ego keeps no careful eye on time,
the hours simply vanish exploring the sublime.

The two come together in their little wooden house
and find their consummation with the spider and the mouse.
Triple-hinged the door reveals a different world within
smelling of beeswax, petrol, tarpaulin.

How I should like to be a woodlouse in the dark
and see the private man in the shed's generous heart,
feel the hand- stroked weather board, every splinter's prick;
hear the tenderness of silence, the roof felt's gentle creak.

A shed's the secret mistress every man desires
in its dark interior they're forgiven all their cares.
Safe in the embrace of moonlit tongue and groove
a shed is the nearest thing many find to love.

FUGUE

American railway magnate Leland Stanford, employed Eadweard Muybridge to settle a bet that a galloping horse's hooves all left the ground at once in what was called unsupported transit. Stanford's wife, who founded the university in her husband's honour, died in mysterious circumstances.

Muybridge, whose original name was Muggeridge, suffered severe head injuries in a stagecoach accident in 1874. Fourteen years later he shot and killed his wife's lover. He pleaded insanity related to his injuries, but he was acquitted by the jury on the grounds that he was justified in killing the man who seduced his wife.

One of Muybridge's friends was an 8' 2" Chinese giant, Chang Woo Gow.

Lo Ping	"This poem is composed of foot notes," says Lo Ping. "The foot is the birthplace of movement."

Mrs Leland Stanford	"I find it hard to write. I'm so distressed by all that's bound me since his death. I use the housekeeping monies the executors provide to keep his dreams alive. I feel like a fraudster. They tell me not to fear, but guilt and fear are my first response to every change I feel. I remain in his shadow, at such a pass..."

Lo Ping	I was not a servant in the Stanford household, I am imagined there. I fly through marble halls warmed by rugs and skins. In the library her husband challenges my sometime friend whose eyes skate towards the windows

Leland Stanford	"Ee – ayed – wierd. That's the strangest name I've ever had the pleasure to annunciate, Mr Maybridge."

Lo Ping	His visitor's eyes ricochet off every edge and surface as if hunting movement unseen by human eyes. "That's My-bridge, Governor Stanford," the Englishman mutters. "Muybridge."

I wear a red silk gown, a hat with a golden tassle
to satisfy the urge for stereotypes. See how,
one arm raised just above my head, I rise,

spin on my axis and fly through air and time
to here, a Coronation Stone in Kingston,
England, a young boy pondering
the Saxon names engraved into the rock.
Aethelstan
Edmund
Eadred
Eadwig
Eadgar
Eadweard the Martyr

The boy's imagining his name's not Muggeridge.

A news reel voice

In his camera shed at Palo Alto
the arrangement of cameras along the path of motion
is pretty much the same as the Brothers Wachowski
will use in *Matrix/Reloaded/Revolutions* for Bullet Time.
Yeun Wo Ping (no relation) choreographed the moves.

Mrs Leland Stanford

The horses fly!
A burly man mounts a stair.
A woman naked from the waist
calls her naked daughter to her.
The tenderness, the illusion,
how touching, how unreal!

The man from
MOVIA/TimeTrack

"We're presently working on a demo
of an 80 camera digital system
which streams uncompressed
high definition images
(1600 x 1200) direct to disk.
In this system each camera's
out of sync with its neighbour
by exactly 1/80th of the frame rate
(so each frame-cycle is divided evenly
amongst the 80 cameras).
The result will be a constant circular
virtual camera move which does
a complete 360 approximately
every three seconds (80 frames)
at an effective frame rate of up to
1200 frames per second."

Lo Ping	Lo Ping knows that horses fly, that concubines catch fire, that the wood in the stock farm fence was yew, wasn't it?

Frame by frame
you change yourself.
Muggeridge to
Muygridge to
Muybridge to
misunderstandings,
mispronunciations
What did you expect?
Honour? Deference?

You're out of time, mad as an Apache,
unsupported, high on a jutting projection
above thin air. Branding, communication,
the power of names, of reinvention,
reassigned identity, gender, race, species.

When we run the sequence forward do rivers really dry up,
seas overwhelm people who overwhelm nature non-stop?
Can redemption ever be more than absorption, more
than a drift to homogeny's soup, more than the mean
of everything mean? The pictures run on, a flutter of cards
splayed through the air. Good God, have you seen this?
Children are fitted with chemical implants to improve
the interface between man and machine. But only some
children. The rest gang in silhouette on the periphery
chanting their hunger, shouldering guns. System assisted
the cultured are killers or connive in the killing which is
much the same thing.

Eadweard Muybridge	I'm unhinged to the point that I would leave my leavings. I slip between before and after. In a fugue, I fugue, turn back to where I started. One moment we were on the road to Denver, as smart as fish, the next we're upturned in a ditch, a wheel is spinning, a man is dead, the horses run and run with flailing reins. I feel dragged to my right, and cannot rise.

I am a wounded insect on the trail. The eyes
in my puppet head see everything anew
and for a moment, in a dream, I watch
the horses fly. A tortured day and then
another tortured night I lie in pain
from which is born my longing, to see
my place of birth again. Kingston, the borough
royal, the town of kings, the kings' stone.

Is there redemption in return? Can a child
reclaim its mother's lost embrace? Her
movements? The spreading of a father's
vanished smile? The brother's tender play?
Must all animation be cursed by stillness?
These thoughts mingled with my dream
of flying horses as my body tried to pull
itself together, a broken marionette.

Denied that locomotion we take for granted
I began the journey back to where I started.
I had to learn how to put one foot ahead
the other. I began to think again.
For five years I was a fugitive from life,
from my science, from America.
I hid in my history, an unsupported flight,
finding myself finding myself in Kingston.

During those months of eerie reverie,
of being yet being forgotten, I often
walked to the Coronation Stone
memorial to the Saxon Kings. This
perambulation and their names
affected me. The rhythm of the walk
helped restore me, the soundings
of the names cast a baptismal spell.

So it was that in my place of birth
I conceived my own rebirth as
Eadweard Muybridge.

THE FOREST RIDGE

I

By dusk, the thunderclouds pile high above the Weald,
the forecast is for storms across the whole South East.
A hobby glides the thermals scanning for its prey
and all below's connected in its piercing eye –
a hilly trek of meadows, woods, a sandstone ridge,
the English landscape quilted to its vision's edge.
Thin ponds like molten metal, gleam with evening light;
great houses cast their shadows on gardens open late;
secluded steep ravines are coursed by narrow streams
as ancient tracks and droveways wander through the trees.
Disaster's harbinger or herald of new thought,
the raptor wheels, plummets with a Spitfire's art
and snatches from the sky an unsuspecting swift,
reminding any watcher of its warlike craft
of other battles won and lost on this unique terrain.
And battles yet to come, perhaps? Between the town
and country, the old urban/rural split? More roads,
More telecoms? More houses? More desired goods?
The loss of rural industry and local style?
Endangered habitats? Initiatives that fail?
The mission creep of humans on wilderness' edge,
environmental damage with public interest's badge?
A Spanish hacienda encroaches on a wood,
that's grubbed up by its owner; then the widened road
puts more earth under tarmac, more cars on the move...
Not one the hobby's concern, drifting high above.

II

Down on the ground some people see things differently
and in their different bodies question constantly
accepted lines, the shrug of couldn't give a damn.
They challenge complacency's attitude to change.
What if a kind of partnership could link people
to their land? If the High Weald Forest Ridge could pull
itself together, forests in a sisterhood,
as midwives to a reborn sense of place, the thread
to link Ashdown, St Leonards, Waterdown and Worth,
the largest tract of wooded country in the south?
And what could be achieved? What poise and balance found
between the many different claims upon the land,
involving all in their landscape's heritage
of any capability, background or age?
How many barriers could be removed? How
could folk be empowered, as the jargon goes, so
that they can make a difference? Skills and crafts relearnt?
Gardening to nurture wildlife? Can do, not can't?

III

Over barn and milestone, church and riverbank,
war memorial, fingerpost, fly-tipped junk,
across the Ridge the questions hover like the dusk,
each question represents an issue and a task.
People and creatures, plants and birds, the land itself
and history wait for an answer, all breathing held.
The ghosts of iron masters stand beside their ponds.
Pond-dipping children sift the future in their hands.
The gills and meadows, parks and heaths all teem with life –
brown hare and pipistrelle, emerald dragonfly,
hay scented buckler fern, sundew, bog asphodel;
the yellow meadow ant, roe deer and water vole,
The settlements that sparkle in the dusk and drape
the Forest Ridge with traceries of light and hope,
and the country in between where blackbirds sing,
are woven together in myth, story and song,
all interconnected, nothing stands alone.
The one in the many, the many in the one.

FOOTWORK

Butterfly hunt

After the painting by Berthe Morisot

A whispering draft. Birdsong.
A cabbage white stops on the painter's nose.
Her sister's in two minds, may smile.
The little girl will point, certainly.

Her brother, who has no truck with butterflies,
fingers his guitar. In the arbor, his aunt canoodles
with her lover, a Monsieur Bleriot. Birdsong.
No one hears the gathering in the woods.

Earth moving equipment

They're in two minds to rise or fall,
burp or fart. Our JCBs have bitten
off more than they can chew. Their
eyes are bigger than their tummies.
Their jaws are bigger than their brains.
They've gorged themselves on earth
and just can't move. I think, says one,
I could manage one more mouthful.

The secret room

The priest hole or the attic loft
the hidden vault in Lara Croft
the car, the van, the tent, the mine,
the wooden horse, the desert shrine.

The toilet and the garden shed
the box room with the squeaky bed
the mouse hole or the monster's lair
the catacomb, the trickster's snare.

The gaol, the camera or the page
the space lab or the diver's cage
the baby's cot, the dying bed
the weird stuff inside your head.

The office on the thirteenth floor
the ancient slab, the antique door
Incubator, pulsing womb,
torture chamber, mummy's tomb.

The space we thought was ours alone
built of air or solid stone
The secret chamber we all share
yet never meet each other there.

Another secret room

Changing in M & S.
        The little cubicle
in that sauna.
        The ante room
in Warsaw
where Uzis watched over
the dealings Steve and I
had with the girls.
        The office
on Northampton station
where no one could identify
him, or his disease.
        The theatre
where they took away his
meningococcal leg.
        The loft
where Richard kept his
magazines.
        The garage
where someone
lit that jar of petrol.
        The place
I always go
and never tell a soul.
        The bog
where the bouncers caught me
with a urinal in my arms.
        The cell
the coppers gave me.
        The shed
where a stranger
did something to my brother
and sent us home with giant sticks
of rhubarb for my mother
        Upstairs
in Marylebone
for those 50 minute sessions
Later in the curry house
Utterly none the wiser
utterly none the wiser
in my secret room
In my secret room

Secret moves

The hand beneath the table
The gun between the lips
The car parked in the lay-by
The passing lights of ships

The door softly closing
The corner of the mouth
The parcel in the litter bin
The bomber from the south

The last click of the tumbler
The opening of flowers
The signature of ghosts
The flight path to the towers

The well worn track of habit
The meandering of silt
The hand in the other's pocket
The tidal flow of guilt

The galaxy exploding
The way ideas move
The sap inside the first new shoot
The secret moves of love.

Messages sent in early spring after a long winter

On a starlit night
In the night sky above Porthcurno,
we watch a comet, its tail of breath.
The sky is ebony. Stars pierce our eyes,
the wind scything the wires.
The old brick fireplace; in its hearth
red hot coals radiate their warmth
around our family group: mother,
father, sons, daughters, dog.

A photograph of the neatest man in Somerset
The withies are bound like trolls in stooks.
Within their sheltering arbour he grinds
the blade, the whetstone held daintily,
little pinky crooked with reason –
a blade this sharp will cut a finger
neatly to a stump. His was
the neatest blade. It lies unsharpened
on the mantelpiece; next to the bottle.

To friends arriving from a distance
No. We've not gone to any great trouble.
Is it really that long? It's hard to believe
it's over ten years since the birthday party
in Letchworth and that unfortunate situation.
We've tried to get to the bottom of things,
many times, without success. You'll find us easily.
The road is full of petals, cherry blossom
blown like snow drifts; our world of pink.

A son's first trip by plane
He sat in his seat as if glued in,
little legs almost straight, looking
straight ahead, lips pressed together
in a determined reverie. He accepted every gift
of headphones, magazine, young flyer's fun bag
and listened intently to Channel 3 as he flew,
but never moved; much like the plane
which remained firmly at its Gatwick stand.

To a man walking a railway

Counting the sleepers helps the time pass more quickly,
except at night when it's best to sleep in the tunnels.
The trains here are irregular, if they ever arrive at all,
so you need have no fear of sudden expresses.
Do you spit on the rail shine? Do you suffer a mirage
of destinations? That the line ends somewhere?
Out in the country you can enjoy the horizons,
the wind's generosity with petals. Believe me.

A visit to the walled city

Lilac and jasmine surround the citadel
its pavements of gravel flecked by gold lichen
the only gateway black in the noon shade
huge flags unfurled on its towers. The woman
is brushing her hand on the turret, stroking
the stone as if its alive. She flinches
the moment the crust of the gargoyle splits,
revealing her mother's dangerous eyes.

A man turned to stone

The sky is charcoal, stabbed by stars.
On the high cliff of cloud he rests
his chin upon his knee, clutches
his head in despair, weighed down by the vacancy
beneath him. His hands frame his eyes
that stare into nothingness, full of pain.
He sees nothing, except imprisonment, freefall.
Petrified, no parachute, he dare not move.

Ignominious: on the comic and the tragic

On Thursday, a young mountaineer fell
and swung in space calling for help.
The calls got fainter and fainter until
they finally ceased on Friday morning.
There's something about that movement,
like a pendulum. Funny, sad, funny...

Acknowledgements

'Clothes of Grey' was read at the graveside of Slovenian poet Srečko Kosovel (1904-1926) on Sunday October 1st 2006 as part of a short series of readings by attendees at the Apokalypse Review in Review meeting, Dane 2006. Meela Veeren, my niece, died on September 24th 2006 aged 22.

'Earthed' was written as a response to a photograph by Margaret Weller LBIPP as part of the Footwork event at The Crypt Gallery, Seaford in December 2004.

'Mapping the body', 'Auscultation' and 'Puppet workshop' were written as part of *From the Outside In*, a Shedman residency at East Sussex Healthcare Trust with visual artist Sue Ridge supported by Arts in Healthcare.

'Hawkish' was written as part of a project working with Arundel Writers Group and Arun Artists.

'Perspective' was written as a response to the work of Victor Stuart Graham as part of the Footwork event at The Crypt gallery Seaford in December 2005.

'Pink Cavalier' was written for performance as part of Footwork's Secret Moves.

'Fish out of Water' and 'The Singing Fish' were first performed with a musical accompaniment by Phil Roberts and have been published in *Dreaming Beasts* (Krebs and Snopes, 2005). With acknowledgement to Al Green, Teenie Hodges, Bobby McFerrin and Gloria Gaynor.

'Shedgang', 'Reflections' and 'Mr Booth's Shed' were written as part of the ArchiTEXTS residency at the Booth Museum of Natural History in Brighton, curated by Mark Hewitt.

'Ian's Cousin's Grandad's Shed' was written during the Shedman residency at the Appledore Visual Arts Festival.

'Halloween', 'Individual' and 'Dragon' were first published in *The Shed* magazine.

'Maximum Shed' was written as a special commission for Jonathan Bridgeman for his oldest friend Max to mark the opening of his new shed.

'Two in One' was read on *Gardeners' World* on BBC TV. It was a private commission for a lady whose lover adored his shed and in which they consummated their relationship. She said he was a very different man inside.

'Fugue' was commissioned as part of THE SOUTH's Project Poetry! on the theme place of birth. This commission was based in Kingston, Surrey, birthplace of the photographer and movie pioneer Eadweard Muybridge.

'The Forest Ridge' was written as a commission from the High Weald AONB Unit. It uses the alexandrine form of Michael Drayton's Poly-Olbion (1622) which itself bemoaned the changes to the Weald four hundred years ago.

The poems in Footwork were all written for Footwork events. Many thanks to all the other Footworkers – Tim Beech, Judith Cair, Anne Collins, Bernadette Cremin, Tom Cunliffe, Martine Large and Robert Walton.

I am very grateful for the support of a personal development grant received from Arts Council England,South East.

With many thanks to Ros Barber, Brendan Cleary, Sasha Dugdale, Anne Marie Fyfe, Ciaran O'Driscoll, Les Robinson and tall-lighthouse, Anne Rouse, David Swann and Jackie Wills.

John Davies published his first pamphlet collection *The Nutter in the Shrubbery* in 2002. In the same year he won an ArchiTEXTS Award for his first residency as Shedman (www.shedman.net). He has also received an Arts Council England personal development award. His poetry has been published in anthologies and magazines and he has read his work at events and festivals in the UK, Ireland and Europe. John founded and was director of literary arts organisation THE SOUTH from 2002-07.